Writer's TOOLBOX

Show Me a Story

Writing Your Own Picture Book

Includes all letters except V

ALPHABET

PICTURE WINDOW BOOKS
Minneapolis, Minnesota

by Nancy Loewen

illustrated by Christopher Lyles

Editor: Jill Kalz
Designers: Nathan Gassman and Matt Bruning
Page Production: Melissa Kes
Editorial Director: Nick Healy
The illustrations in this book were created
with mixed media on illustration board.

Picture Window Books
151 Good Counsel Drive
P.O. Box 669
Mankato, MN 56002-0669
877-845-8392
www.picturewindowbooks.com

Printed in the United States of America.

All books published by Picture Window Books
are manufactured with paper containing
at least 10 percent post-consumer waste.

Library of Congress Cataloging-in-Publication Data
Loewen, Nancy, 1964–
Show me a story : writing your own picture book /
by Nancy Loewen ; illustrated by Christopher Lyles.
p. cm. — (Writer's Toolbox)
Includes index.
ISBN 978-1-4048-5341-6 (library binding)
ISBN 978-1-4048-5342-3 (paperback)
1. Picture books for children—Authorship.
I. Lyles, Christopher, 1977- II. Title.
PN147.5.L64 2009
808.06'8—dc22   2008040588

Special thanks to our adviser, Terry Flaherty, Ph.D., Professor of English,
Minnesota State University, Mankato, for his expertise.

There are many kinds of picture books. Some are nonfiction. They give us facts about real things. Others are fiction. They tell stories from the author's imagination.

Most picture books are written by one person and illustrated by another. We won't be learning much about illustrations in this book. For now, it's all about the writing.

Our example, *WEBSTER'S WISH*, is a work of fiction. Read the story first. Then go back to page 5 and start learning about the many tools authors use to put stories like this together.

Webster's Wish

Webster knew the alphabet backward and forward.

He liked all the letters—except for one. V.

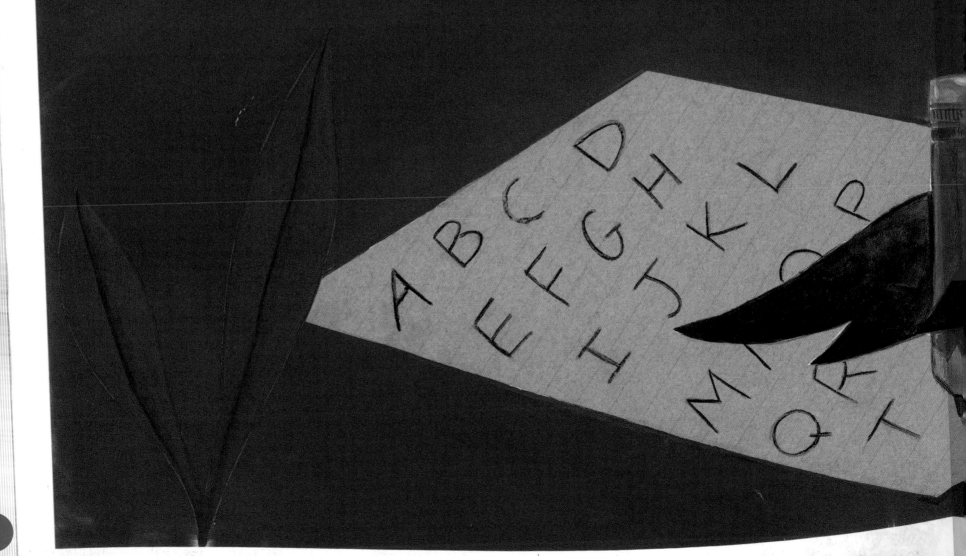

~ Tool 1 ~

Stories can be divided into three parts: the **BEGINNING**, the middle, and the ending. The beginning is the start of the story.

~ Tool 2 ~

In most picture books, two basic things happen in the beginning. First, we meet the main **CHARACTER**. Characters are the people, animals, or creatures in the story. The main character is the one character who appears most often.

~ Tool 3 ~

Second, we get a hint of a **PROBLEM** or struggle that will shape the story. Here we meet Webster and learn that he doesn't like the letter V.

~ Tool 4 ~

In the beginning of the story, we also learn where and when the story takes place. This is called the **SETTING**.

~ Tool 5 ~

In a picture book, the **ILLUSTRATIONS** will tell part of the story. For example, the setting for *Webster's Wish* is the outdoors, on the ground and in the sky, over a stretch of warm, nearly cloudless days. The words of the story don't tell us this. The illustrations show us.

Oh, V was all right for spelling words like *view* and *valentine* and *vamoose*. And it was certainly a fine choice for the word *love*.

Webster just didn't want to **FLY** in a **V** shape all the time.

He went to Sir Graybill, the leader of the flock. Sir Graybill, of course, flew at the very tip of the V.

"Can't we try a different letter?" Webster pleaded. "Can't we do something new?"

Sir Graybill considered Webster's request. He gazed at the other geese. He squinted into the sky.

~ Tool 6 ~

In good picture books, **PROBLEM-SOLVING** happens when the characters take action. But the problem isn't solved right away. Here Webster goes to the leader of the flock with his letter problem. Will Sir Graybill say yes?

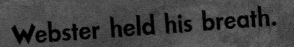

Webster held his breath.

Finally Sir Graybill shook his head. "Some of the geese would be afraid to fly in a new letter shape," he said. "The V is all they have known. They might get confused. No, a new letter might lead to trouble."

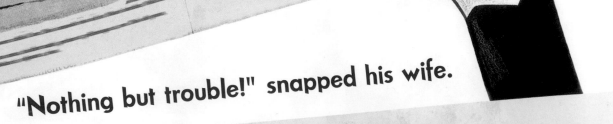

~ Tool 7 ~

DIALOGUE is what your characters say to each other. Good dialogue does lots of things. It tells us more about what the characters are like. It helps move the story along. It gives the reader information. And it's a great way to make your characters come alive on the page.

New Letter a Disaster

"Nothing but trouble!" snapped his wife.

Webster walked glumly away. But he didn't stop dreaming of other letters. What would it feel like to fly in a complicated K? Or a curvy C? Or—he shuddered with delight—a swirling, soaring S?

The way characters feel can be just as important as what they do. We see that Webster is sad. And we remember what it's like to feel let down. Because we feel what Webster is feeling, we care more about what happens to him.

During grazing time, Webster scratched letters in the dirt. He made A's and J's, D's and Z's, I's and Y's.

~ Tool 8 ~

The main part of the story is called the **MIDDLE**. In the beginning, we were introduced to Webster and his problem. Now we're going to find out what he does to solve that problem.

~ Tool 9 ~

The things that happen in a story are called the **PLOT**. Each event should be connected in some way to the one before it.

"What a dreamer," chuckled one goose.

"Yeah," said another. "We should be PROUD of our V's."

"Our V's are perfect," a third goose said. "Not just any bird can fly in a V. It takes real skill to do what we do."

"That's true," Webster admitted. But he went on dreaming of R's, T's, and Q's.

One afternoon, a goose named Twigs waddled over to him.

"What?" Webster asked crossly. "Are you going to put me down, too?"

"Not at all," Twigs said. "We've been watching you, Webster. You leave a trail of letters wherever you go. And some of us are starting to see things your way. Our V's are great, but a little variety never hurt anyone."

The other geese clucked and nodded.

Webster grinned. "In that case, I call to order the first meeting of the New Letter Crew!"

17

Together, the geese scratched more letters in the dirt. Carefully they considered each one. They argued. They laughed. They giggled and groaned.

~ Tool 11 ~

Picture books can show events in two ways. A **SCENE** is like taking a video camera and hitting the record button. Things happen right in front of the reader.

~ Tool 12 ~

In **SUMMARY**, time is pressed together. The reader gets an idea of what happened, but doesn't know the details.

This part of the story is summary. We don't know what the geese are saying. And that's OK. All we need to know is that they are working together. The summary quickly gets us to the next part of the plot.

19

When they came to a certain letter near the end of the alphabet, they all had the same idea at once.

"Well, knock me over with a feather!" Webster exclaimed. "I can't believe I didn't think of this sooner!"

"We can do this," Twigs said.
"We can really do this!"

~ Tool 13 ~

Sometimes the reader knows something that the characters don't know. Sometimes the characters know something that the reader doesn't know. This builds **SUSPENSE**. Here Webster and the New Letter Crew have made a discovery. But we haven't been told what it is.

21

The New Letter Crew went to tell the others. Soon all the geese were nodding, even the old-timers.

"We'll practice right now," announced Sir Graybill. "We'll fly over to Farmer Cap's pond. Gather around, everyone, and number off by two's."

"It will lead to nothing but trouble!" warned Sir Graybill's wife. But in all the excitement, no one paid any attention to her.

The suspense builds! We still don't know what the geese have in mind. But the warning from Sir Graybill's wife makes us wonder if the plan will go smoothly.

The takeoff was confusing. Geese flapped, bumped, and bumbled in the air.

And then—

There it was!

A little willy-nilly at first ...

~ Tool 14 ~

What exactly are the geese doing? We still don't know, but we're getting closer and closer to finding out. The most exciting moment in a story is called the **CLIMAX**.

And a bit wobbly ...

But very definitely ...

a

w!

~ Tool 15 ~

A good **ENDING** should answer the questions that were raised during the story. The ending shouldn't be rushed. But it shouldn't be dragged out, either. The reader should feel pleased. Webster tried something new, and his idea worked!

26

Let's Review!

These are the **15 tools** you need to write great picture books.

The BEGINNING **(1)** of a picture book introduces the main CHARACTER **(2)** and the PROBLEM **(3)** that will move the story. Where and when the story takes place is called the SETTING **(4)**. In a picture book, ILLUSTRATIONS **(5)** share the storytelling duties with the text. Not everything in the text will be shown in the pictures. Not everything in the pictures will be explained in the text.

Characters take action to SOLVE THEIR PROBLEMS **(6)**. Good DIALOGUE **(7)** gives the reader information and moves the story along.

The MIDDLE **(8)** of the story is where most of the action takes place. The story's events are called the PLOT **(9)**. Every event should add to the overall story. At the TURNING POINT **(10)**, readers start to believe that the characters just might solve their problems. Events can be shown as SCENES **(11)** or SUMMARY **(12)**.

SUSPENSE **(13)** can move a story forward. It keeps the reader turning the pages. What will happen next? The suspense builds until the reader reaches the most exciting moment in the story, the CLIMAX **(14)**. The reader should feel pleased with the ENDING **(15)** of a picture book. The questions that came up during the story should be answered.

Getting Started Exercises

- Characters in picture books can be anything. They can be people, animals, or even objects like lamps or cheese. Think of a character, and figure out what he or she is like. What are some things your character does well? What are your character's weaknesses? Who are your character's friends? When you feel you know your character, ask yourself: What sort of problems might this character have? If you've got a character and a problem, you've got the start of a story!

- Talk to your parents, relatives, friends, teachers, and babysitters. Since stories come from problems, ask them to describe their "worst of" moments: worst meals, vacations, birthday presents, sports events, holidays, and so on. Could any of these moments be turned into a story?

- Keep a notebook handy, and write down the things that catch your attention. Maybe it's a faucet that dripped all night or the way your school smells on a hot day. After awhile, you'll have lots of notes. Some of these might be the starting point of a picture book.

Writing Tips

 The best way to learn how to write a picture book is to read lots of them. Then read them again and again! Take notes. What do you like most about them?

 Picture books don't have a lot of words, so every word counts. One word that fits is far better than several words that aren't quite right.

 Read your work out loud. Do you stumble over certain words or sentences? See what you can change to make your story easier to read.

 Draw boxes on a piece of paper to stand for each page of your book. Write a few words or draw a small picture to show what is on each page. This is called a "dummy." A dummy will help you "see" your story.

Glossary

beginning—the first of three main story parts; the start

character—a person, animal, or creature in a story

climax—a story's most exciting moment

dialogue—the words spoken between two or more characters; in writing, dialogue is set off with quotation marks

ending—the last of three main story parts; the finish

events—things that happen

fiction—written works about characters and events that aren't real

illustrations—artwork that shows scenes from a story

middle—the second of three main story parts; where the action happens

nonfiction—written works about real people and events

plot—what happens in a story

problem—something that causes trouble

request—to ask for something

scenes—events shown as they happen

setting—the time and place of a story

summary—events shown as though time is pressed together

suspense—worry, unease

turning point—the moment at which a change happens

To Learn More

More Books to Read

Bemelmans, Ludwig. *Madeline.* New York: Puffin Books, 1998.

Bullard, Lisa. *You Can Write a Story! A Story-Writing Recipe for Kids.* Minnetonka, Minn.: Two-Can Publishing, 2007.

Madden, Kerry. *Writing Smarts: A Girl's Guide to Writing Great Poetry, Stories, School Reports, and More!* Middleton, Wis.: Pleasant Co., 2002.

Sendak, Maurice. *Where the Wild Things Are.* New York: HarperCollins, 1991.

On the Web

FactHound offers a safe, fun way to find educator-approved Internet sites related to this book.

Here's what you do:
1. Visit *www.facthound.com*
2. Choose your grade level.
3. Begin your search.

This book's ID number is 9781404853416

Index

Look for all of the books in the Writer's Toolbox series:

Once Upon a Time: Writing Your Own Fairy Tale
Show Me a Story: Writing Your Own Picture Book
Sincerely Yours: Writing Your Own Letter
Words, Wit, and Wonder: Writing Your Own Poem